A Handful of Shiulis

Poems by
Avijeet Das

Clare Songbirds Publishing House Chapbook Series
ISBN 978-1-947653-09-2
Clare Songbirds Publishing House
A Handful of Shiulis© 2017 Avijeet Das
All Rights Reserved. Clare Songbirds Publishing House retains right to reprint.
Permission to reprint individual poems must be obtained from the author who owns the copyright.

Printed in the United States of America
FIRST EDITION

Clare Songbirds Publishing House Mission Statement:
Clare Songbirds Publishing House was established to provide a print forum for the creation of limited edition, fine art from poets and writers, both established and emerging. We strive to reignite and continue a tradition of quality, accessible literary arts to the national and international community of writers, and readers. We support our literary artists with high quality services and on-going support. Chapbook manuscripts and art quality poetry broadsides are carefully chosen for their ability to propel the expansion of art and ideas in literary form. We provide an accessible way to promote the art of words in order to resonate with, and impact, readers not yet familiar with the siren song of poets and writers. Clare Songbirds Publishing House espouses a singular cultural development where poetry creates community and becomes commonplace in public places.

Clare Songbirds Publishing House
140 Cottage Street
Auburn, New York 13021
www.ClareSongbirdspub.com

Contents

Sylvia Plath and Me	7
Sunrises and Sunsets	8
Last Night	9
I Heard the Breeze	10
Mrignaynee (Doe-eyed)	11
After Seeing You	12
Sundari Jaal (She is the water-fall)	13
Oh Layla	14
I found you	15
Sea-shore	16
I Will Wait	17
Dirty boots	18
Conversations with Sylvia	19
And We will Meet	20
She is the Zahir	21
The Charm is in Waiting	22
Mademoiselle	23
Let's Sleep	24
Aching	25
Flaming Moon	27
Morning Waltz	28
Precious Flowers	30
Tender Breeze	31
She Still Teaches	32
Jacaranda	33
Darkness	34
Wandering	35
Beethoven	36
I Am No Writer	37
September Sky	39

Acknowledgements:

Sylvia Plath and me - *EastLit Journal*, January, 2016
Sundari Jal (She is the Waterfall) - *Story Mirror*, 2016
Sea-shore – "First of the Fourth" *aaduna*, April 2017.
I Will Wait – *Hello Poetry*, 2016
Aching - *Poem Hunter*, 2014
Flaming Moon - *Poem Hunter*, 2014
Morning Waltz - *Hall Of Poets Magazine*, July, 2015
Precious Flowers - *Word Wine* poetry anthology, March, 2014.

To all the Poetry lovers of the world. The people who love to read poetry, write poetry, or the people who just love to listen to poetry. You are the ones who make this world a better place by your sensitivity and tenderness. You are the ones who inspire the future generations to live, let live and spread love and happiness.

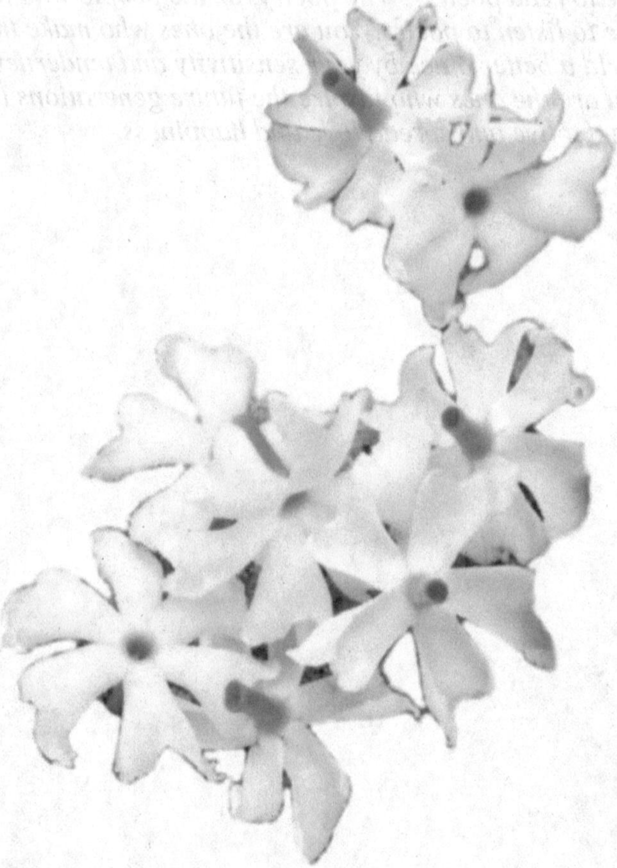

Sylvia Plath and Me

Sylvia Plath and me
Met a long time ago,
A really long, long time ago,
I think it was a beautiful winter day,
No, a November morning,
Time stood still that much I know!

Her words they stung me,
Pulled me high,
Her thoughts unknown rays
Golden and silvery
Darting about in myriad directions,
Commanded me to follow,
Enraptured in them, I flew with my mind's cockpit!

Her words, they engulfed me,
Hovering in my days
And sailing in my nights's dreams
On a yacht to a faraway island,
Marooned, heart-wrecked!
My mornings would awoken
With a resplendent love,
A warm after-glow,
A radiance just sublime!

Today her words still boomerang
In my days and in my nights
When the cricket's shrill cries reverberate
But my mind only listens to Sylvia's words,
Her thoughts, the magic of darting about
In unknown directions!
Sigh!

Sunrises and Sunsets

Sunrises and sunsets were breathtaking
Moments in his life,
Moments of exhilaration and ecstasy,
Deeply moving moments
When he would dream
Dreams that splashed
Myriad colors on his mind's gray canvas!

Last Night

When I think of you,
I feel fragrance
When I think of our conversations,
I feel alive
My days smile
And my nights sparkle

Last night
When I crashed into
My stupid, empty bed,
I took off all your inhibitions
From the realm of surrealism
And I surrendered my soul
To your soul!

I heard the breeze...

I heard the breeze whisper your name to the trees
And the flowers giggled smiling at the leaves
I and my loneliness keep talking about you.

Mrignaynee

Thy visage epitomizes the
Transcendence of timeless beauty
If only thy eyes flutter once
The bees lose their direction
And the breeze its rain

Thy eyes hold countless stars
Yet to be discovered
If only thy eyelashes flicker once
The ships forget their navigation
And the fighting men their aim

Oh Mrignaynee
Thy one glance has the power
To enslave proud men
From Afghanistan to America
India to Spain

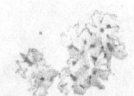

After seeing you…

Even after seeing you a thousand times
Why is there this ache within my heart?

Sundari Jaal (She is the Water-fall)

She is the giver
She flows with pristine love
Cascading on the rocks

She is the lover
She loves with candor
Mingling with the sand

She is an enigma
A mystery forever
Yet to be solved

She is the enslaver
Charming the plants, trees,
Butterflies and bees

She is the empress
Coming down from her abode
To nurture her land.

Oh Layla

Some words were left unsaid Oh Layla,
As you slept peacefully in my arms,
And the stars kept on peeping into the room
to glance at your smile!

I found you...

In the silence of the ticking of the clock's minute hand,
                I found you
In the echoes of the reverberations of time,
                I found you
In the tender silence of the long summer night,
                I found you
In the fragrance of the rose petals,
                I found you
In the orange of the sunset,
                I found you
In the blue of the morning sky,
                I found you
In the pitter-patter of the falling raindrops,
                I found you
In the echoes of the mountains,
                I found you
In the green of the valleys,
                I found you
In the chaos of this world,
                I found you
In the turbulence of the oceans,
                I found you
In the shrill cries of the grasshopper at night,
                I found you
In the gossamer sublimity of the silken cobweb,
                I found you

Sea-shore

A strange feeling of loneliness
Adrift near the blue canvas
You may stare long and listen deep
Yet not know whether sea-shore or sea-snore!

Conch shells tickling toes
Crabs playing hide-and-seek in the sand
Tea-sellers doing brisk business
While the coconut-sellers practice playing their
Baja and band!

That old man over there
Is selling trinkets made of stones
That old woman the entire world
In a map without any hole!

You may follow the footsteps
The whole day will pass
With you going around in circles
Yet not reaching anywhere at last!

The balloon seller looks happy
Selling blue, yellow, green and red
Yet no meal has made to his stomach
After yesterday's evening- shade!

The children always enjoy with a mad frenzy
Their dogs happily biting their own tails
The mothers keep smiling and encouraging
While their fathers aloof in their own minds
Lonely lane!

The fakirs always throng the sea-shore
To find meaning in the chaos
And then they too become melancholy
Feeling nothing but their naked toes.

Wait for you...

And I will wait for you
Like the leaves
For their rain…

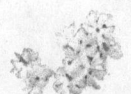

Dirty Boots

My boots are
Soiled and dirty
From all the walking
That I did!

Last night
I was a mad man
Searching for a whiff
Of your Fragrance!

The stars and the moon
Even laughed at me!

Conversations

We have conversations most nights, Sylvia Plath and me
On these cold wintry nights with our coffee mugs in hand,
We talk for hours and hours, Sylvia Plath and me
We sit on the terrace and look at the stars and the moon,
Sylvia Plath and me
We talk about books, movies
and a thousand and one things

She loves the mountains just as I do
She day-dreams just as I do
She is addicted to her solitude just as I am
She loves watching the rain-drops fall slowly on to the
green leaves of an old guava tree just as I do
She loves drifting in time and time travel just as I do
She loves looking at the waves dashing against the rocks
just as I do
We have conversations most nights, Sylvia Plath and me.

And we will meet

And we will meet in the woods
Far far away from this hustle and bustle
And share love and sunshine…

She is the Zahir

Like a splendid mosaic of myriad colors,
She in all her hues of sensitivity would paint her feelings
In your mind's gray skies
She was the butterfly making you run after her
She was the Zahir,
A mirage that transcended
Borders and time-zones

The Charm is in waiting...

The charm is in waiting...
The fragrance of a hope...
The sublimity of a dream...
The eloquence of a silence...
The resplendence of darkness...
The heat of winter...
The cold of summer...
The flashback of a memory...
The unliving of a moment...

Mademoiselle!

So Mademoiselle, who are you tonight?
A lace masquerade
Or a bluestocking
A parade of colors
Or green with envy
A subtle of satin
Or yellow polka-dots
A labyrinthine maze
Or a serious brown study
A raw Zulu dance
Or fiery red flames
A brown deck of spades
Or a silly tickled pink,
An Intriguing snakes and ladders
Or a sparkling white radiance
A magical gypsy caravan
Or a dark black tragedy
So Mademoiselle, who are you tonight?
Or are you the poet's rhythm and rhyme?

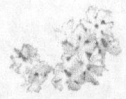

Let's sleep…

Let's sleep
you on top of me
my hands circling your waist
yours holding my face
my legs entangled in yours
yours tenderly wrapped in mine
my eyes staring longingly at yours
yours looking deeply into mine
and we will keep searching for our footsteps
in the sands of time…

Aching...

My whole body
Craving to touch you
Longing to feel you
Pining to hold you
Yearning to hug you
Aching to love you...

Flaming Moon

Moon stops a while glides motionless,
twinkling stars hide and seek in silent glee,
Soft sweet summer breeze gently rustles,
fragrance of lavender wafts in the innocent air,
black night dances along unfolding tenderly,

Listening to the silent song of the night,
we lay together on the grass delightfully,
her head nestling on my arm,
her hands clasping my shirt tightly,
she moves a bit tenderly,
enraptured in some beautiful dream,
sweet summer breeze flows along, caressing tenderly,

She stirs a bit, awakens slowly,
smiling shyly beautiful doe eyes look into mine,
our hands touch, silky skin in radiant glow,
we turn lips touching, slowly and delicately,
she sighs, comes closer, snuggling in once again,
beautiful black night dances along, lingering tenderly.

Morning Waltz

Warm rays of the Sun entered the room silently,
Hovered around the space where I stay,
The gentle fragrance of dew on grass wafted near me,
I was dreaming of a beautiful island,
Surrounded by blue butterflies and red roses
Suddenly waking up,
I found the disarray choking me slowly,
The bed-sheet was rumpled and twisted
in a strange elliptical form,
The pillow was convoluted
into an unknown geometrical shape,
And the quilt had tumbled onto the ground
like a sack of potatoes!
I sat up on bed and rubbed my eyes a little
that is when I saw the pigeon
sitting in the far corner near the door!
Disbelief engulfed me in unknown ways and forms
I rubbed my eyes a few more times
there, the sweet little bird was looking at me
with the brightest of eyes!
I was transfixed by its simple behavior
and she seemed like she had taken a fancy to my room.
Tip-toeing slowly like a ballerina
she went onto my old wooden desk
then she fluttered onto my chair
and glanced around the books.
Couldn't ask her what authors she liked
as I was still in a daze
But she looked happy around the books I could tell;
She had a gentle demeanor and a sweet smile;
Her smile I reflect now is more sublime
than the Mona Lisa smile!
She first took a fancy to Harper Lee;
'To Kill A Mockingbird' she went near to
and gave me a sardonic smile,
I was stupefied beyond my wildest dreams
to even think for a second!
Then she fluttered around 'Macbeth' for over an hour
and kept on glancing at me;

Shakespeare must be smiling in his grave, I chuckled!
Then she got into the mood for a slow dance,
Walked a few steps to the left,
Walked a few steps to the right,
Fluttered in the air with a charming grace,
In perfect synchronized steps,
The dance steps of a beautiful Moonlight Waltz!
(Only the Moon was missing, I realized much later)

I just couldn't take my eyes off her
Graceful to the core, she was a true artist
Mesmerized me completely by her dance
What a presence she had!
Enslaving audiences worldwide for sure, I thought!
And her originality was spellbinding!
Like a trapeze artist she balanced and maneuvered
Danced around the whole stage, like a ballerina she did
(Madonna would pale in her presence, I reflected!)
The exhilaration, the fascination, the infatuation
went on for a full three hours,
And then she flew away by the brown window
near to the door,
In a final bow and in a spectacular flourish!

Precious Flowers

She saw me from afar
And came hurried towards me,
Lest the signal turn green,
She held an expected look in her eyes,
Yet a look of deep melancholy,
She looked at me with honest eyes,
Yet a look of deep pain,
With hands dirtied by the grime,
She held the red roses to me,
To me she seemed like a delicate lily,
An innocence floating in the pond,
I couldn't help but buy them flowers,
The most precious that money could ever buy!

Tender Breeze

The traces of that unseen road
Serpentine and drifting into the mountains
The river will be forever shouting
To follow the unseen

Your heart's radiance makes me forget
My melancholy as I drift along
The untrodden path on moonless nights

The burgundy tenderness
Still lingers in the air
When you would be tender, silent and observing,
And I would be drifting!

Your silence travels into the
Deep alleys of the rooms that I walk into
The roofs look at me and acknowledge the silence

Like that night when I was looking at
The moon and the stars
They understood the silence
And the tender breeze brought me your fragrance!

She Still Teaches

She still teaches there the village kids
Below the Mango tree,
on the outskirts of the Gosaikunda village
The River Trishuli flows by with great fervor

She looks lovingly at the Annapurna Mountains
The Annapurna stands firmly inspiring her forever
Strong, silent and unwavering
They both share that unknown bond!

It was a promise that she made many full moons ago
To her dearest mother and father
when they felt great pride
"I will nurture and educate
the poor children of my village"

Till today three hundred full moons have passed,
Marriage proposals come by the dozen,
Denied, they are flung out!

She looks lovingly at River Trishuli
River Trishuli flows by lovingly and deeply,
Nurturing the entire village with care and concern
They both share that unknown bond!

She still teaches there the village kids,
Below the Mango tree,
on the outskirts of the Gosaikunda village
The River Trishuli flows by with great fervor.

Jacaranda

As the leaves fell slowly
From the Jacaranda,
I ran to catch a piece of the sky…

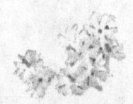

Darkness

Thy dark tresses beseech me
In my days and in my nights
Thy thoughts darker than all charcoal
Lead my mind into an unknown limitless dark expanse

Thy dark eyes beckon me into
The darkest nether world of
Dark galaxies and darker supernovas

Forever in darkness I know no light
Thy dark tresses embalm my dark soul
They dark thoughts sooth my dark being
Thy darkness my dark-light!

Wandering

And I keep wandering
In search of a nothingness…

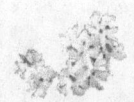

Beethoven

I did put on the record player
The love symphony of Beethoven
Wafted in the air
You and I made love
Last Saturday Afternoon

And the neighbor's dog barked madly
Every time our bed creaked
From all the gyrations
That you and I
Could outmaneuver in our frenzy
Of wanting each other's body
And soul!

I am no writer

I am no writer
Her sparkling eyes made my fingers
write words in the sand,
Her radiant smile made my pen write words in the air,
Her beautiful soul made my typewriter
type poems for eternity,
I am no writer

September Sky

Tonight I miss you like the sky misses his moon
A delicate epiphany growing on grass
 I serenade the breeze into dancing a cha cha cha
The mountains echo in the background
 September sky never looked so charming
Or the sublime petals of the rose more graceful

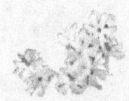

Avijeet Das is a poet and writer from New Delhi in India and currently lives in Kathmandu, Nepal. He is a passionate writer who believes that writing is a necessity for him; it "his mojo." He is an ardent wanderer traveling frequently for work and passion. He is a fervent feminist and a fierce social activist who supports causes relating to women's empowerment, conservation of environment, girl-child education, and equality fo a better world. His work has been published in global magazines, journals, and poetry anthology books. His work has been published by the *East Lit Journal*, *Word Wine* – An Anthology of Contemporary Poetry, *Hall Of Poets* Magazine, Writer's Ezine, *YoAlfaaz*, *Poem Hunter*, *Story Mirror*, *Hello Poetry*, *Poetry Soup* and *aadunna* Literary Magazine.

www.ingramcontent.com/pod-product-compliance
Lightning Source LLC
Chambersburg PA
CBHW012007120526
44592CB00040B/2659